A SOUL INSIDE EACH STONE

poems by

John Tripoulas

DOS MADRES

2016

DOS MADRES PRESS INC.

P.O.Box 294, Loveland, Ohio 45140

www.dosmadres.com   editor@dosmadres.com

Dos Madres is dedicated to the belief that the small press is essential to the vitality of contemporary literature as a carrier of the new voice, as well as the older, sometimes forgotten voices of the past. And in an ever more virtual world, to the creation of fine books pleasing to the eye and hand.

Dos Madres is named in honor of Vera Murphy and Libbie Hughes, the "Dos Madres" whose contributions have made this press possible.

Dos Madres Press, Inc. is an Ohio Not For Profit Corporation and a 501 (c) (3) qualified public charity. Contributions are tax deductible.

Executive Editor: Robert J. Murphy

Illustration & Book Design: Elizabeth H. Murphy
www.illusionstudios.net

Typset in Adobe Garamond Pro & Charlemagne Std.
ISBN 978-1-939929-52-5
Library of Congress Control Number: 2015959767

First Edition

ACKNOWLEDGEMENTS

This small collection took me just over ten years to forge and compile. I would like to thank the following poets and scholars for their support and encouragement during that decade of writing: Aliki Barnstone, Peter Bien, Scott Cairns, Norris Chumley, Stavros Deligiorgis, Theo Dorgan, Edmund Keeley, Paula Meehan, Frederick Naftolin, Anthony Papalas, John Petropoulos, Don Schofield, A.E. Stallings, Nanos Valaoritis and David Young. Special thanks to Robert Murphy, editor at Dos Madres Press, for publishing this collection and to Elizabeth Murphy for her excellent book design and production.

For Leonard Trawick,
master poet, patient mentor.

Table of Contents

I.

VIEW FROM
THE EMERGENCY ROOM

THE FERRY

Winter on the island:
wander in its sorry light,
shiver in the windy damp,
then sit by your calefactor
watching the day's end
over darkening water.
Off to the south coast
as sea, sky and night unite,
a shaky star
bobbles on the horizon—
the ferry's lime prow light.
Next there's stack steam,
bulk of the hull looming,
then the bowstring twang
of hawser lines,
anchor chains rattle,
creaky drawbridge dropping
its hull door, off-loading
provisions to outlast winter:
mail, newsprint, music instruments, contraband.

THE OLIVE PRESS

Trekking on a path
at the outskirts
of the mountain village
where my ancestors once lived—
before me hidden
by overrun shrubs and grasses,
an abandoned olive press.
Within its roofless walls
grows a graveyard cypress
shaped like a taper's flame
and rising twice the height
of the crumbling façade.
In one corner,
a round stone table
balanced on a rock pile frame.
On top of it, smooth, heavy, white,
a barrel-shaped boulder
once fixed to a wooden pole
and drawn round and round
by a donkey to crush the fruit.
Pinned upright to the chimney-wall,
an iron screw press, rusted red,
that mashed the rich brown pulp.
No one from the village
that I asked can remember
when the press last turned.

These are the ruins
of an age-old world,
shaded by a banner of Hades,
where scattered olives
culled under Athena's aegis,
throughout time's turning

turned their lustrous pouring
to an unction of daily life
for food, for light,
for hallowing the dead.
Wordlessly they say to me,
   Trekker, pass by!

INCIDENT ON GREEK INDEPENDENCE DAY

The schoolchildren line up,
to parade on Independence Day
dressed in costumes of yore—
pleated foustanellas, long skirts,
embroidered vests and tasseled caps.
When six lost pigs
wander by and join the procession
the boys and girls take flight,
screaming and dashing,
they hide behind trees
from the friendly swine.
Amongst such chaos
how could liberty reign?
And what about the pigs?
Do they forebode barbarians waiting?
Or are they simply sailors
yearning to break free
from Circe's spell?

IKARIA:
A VIEW FROM THE EMERGENCY ROOM

As ships sail
calmly past an island
famed for a fall,
a ten-year-old playing
tumbles from a wall,
as his parents, nearby,
chat with friends;
the town drunk
pitches down stairs
ripping his skull
into colorful shreds;
six boozed boys
that crashed their bikes
sport starchy casts
on broken bones;
while grandma slips
hoedowning at the feast
and splits her head
like a ripe melon.
People are falling
all over the island.
On the island of Ikaros
they honor his name.

AUTOPSY

Be my guest.
Take what you like.
My heart is yours,
also my guts and bladder.
A slip of the snip, no matter.
There is no other accident.

THE VINEYARD CAFÉ

Step down
three white steps
to roofless walls
crossed with arbor sticks.

Green grape bunches
crown sociable folks
talking and drinking
from old-fashioned cups.

Van Gogh chairs
sway on stone floors
a breeze from the coast
sneaks through the door.

Good Greek food
comes quickly
from the kitchen;
you're far away

so I eat, watch, listen.

FALCONS AT SUNSET

Buoyant, backstroking at early dusk:
there's a brumous half-moon,
transparent thumbprint pasted
to the slate sky when they appear—
black dots focus into sight,
soaring, hovering, diving—
performing aerobatic feats
to feed their chicks nested in the crags
of Ikaria's Atheras mountain.

The Eleonora falcon breeds
on the island's high crests
in colonies of mated pairs,
nest next to nest, begetting
before their fall journey
over the Greek sea
across the Sahara
to the forests of Madagascar.

Black plumed raptors
named for Eleonora,
warrior, heroine, lawgiver
of medieval Sardinia,
Arborea's protector
and protector of the falcons she loved;
her Carta de Longu code
was the law of the land
for four hundred years.

Four hundred years of lawgiving,
five thousand miles of flying…
night comes on,
the birds go back
to the mountainside to roost
and feed their chicks.
I float supine,
arms spread wide, feet fluttering,
watch the sky darken,
the moon become bright.

GARAGE JOCKEY

I live alone
and with the sun
rise like the shade
of a dying laggard.
Time to ring Captain Mimis—
mumble first day words…

After a joke
or the weather report
he'll go down—
roaming Hell's belly
in the dark, the dust,
the lingering gases…

Soon shrieking wheels
burst forth from the serpent's mouth
and dock on Styx bank
where I arrive
with pennies on my eyes.

DOLPHIN

Without expectation or warning
it breached before me:
black, slick-backed
dolphin, epiphany sent
to rouse my torpid heart:

bursting from the waves
along the rocky coast,
near the harbor
where Dionysus
set sail for Naxos.

Rapt by this vision,
in sheer aqua-zoolotry
I cheered and rejoiced
with frenzied shouts
and a wanton dance,

just like the pirates
who plotted theocide,
but bewitched by Dionysus
caroused and turned to dolphins
bounding from their ship's side.

ECHO AND DRUM

Up the footpath,
flowers and cascades
along the mountain flank,
then just ahead
there's the cave door
of a stone chapel.

After quiet petition
in the rock shrine—
my soft words tremble
on saint-painted walls—
it's back to the trail
to continue the climb.

Rising to heights,
I stop at a gorge
sheer on the path-side,
stand at the brink,
shout and wait
for an echo to reply.

There's spectral stillness
after the echo speaks;
then, perhaps affronted
by my reckless cheek
it rouses the beat
of far thunder drums

that muster sheets
of rain to come.
Pelted by raindrops
at first one by one,
time to start
a downhill run—

skirting ditches,
slipping on mud
fleeing across
the mountain face
to escape the deluge
giving chase.

Drubbed by the downpour,
I'm a dripping wretch.
Was it in response
to my grotto prayer
that some power ordained
this tattooing storm?

Or was it for my lip
to an echoing void?
—this baptismal rite,
sacred or mundane,
up on a mountain
drenched by rain?

LATE LAPS ON THE ISLAND

Scratch of soles shifting gravel.
Run-off rain's shoosh to the sea.
Norther crosswind's piercing keen.
Scops owl's call a rhythmic beat:
kew, kew, kew, cues loping feet.

A night plane connects starry dots.
Comets stroke the Milky Way.
Blood moon rising from the bay.
My headlamp picks up distant sparks—
cats' eyes watching in the dark.

When a child at play, I ran—
the child is father to the man!
And now that darkness holds for me
an endless wealth of sound and sight,
I run rejoicing in the night.

WHEN WATER TURNS TO WINE

is the best time
to swim the island bay
and chase an orange sun
that settles in the West.

Cloaked in violet twilight
hides a Maenad's guiding force,
the heartbeat of a holy dance,
limbs glistening in the tide.

A crescent cup smiles
bending toward the bay.
Mother moon pours libation
to her twice-born child.

Ripples chant the divine
in the thaumaturgic sea.
Twisting bobbing rolling diving
drunken currents entwine

like tendrils of a vine
plaiting round a daemon thigh,
this worship in the sacred sea
when water turns to wine.

OCTOPUS

The still surface of the sea
spreads like a soul—

I dive deep
to fathom its secret.

An octopus waits
with arms like spokes
clasping a square stone.

I rise again—
this enfolding, sideways 8
my glimpse of infinity.

PRISM

A prism wreath
surrounds the full moon.
It's the sea salt
on my swim goggles
that scatters the light
to reveal night work
on the floating bridge
of heaven.

At each turn of my head
to breathe with the stroke
I see rainbow colors:
hot orange and red
hem the fringe,
indigo, violet
smooth on the brim.

I lift my mask,
afloat, at rest,
and look up at the moon,
its numinous hues pooled
to a pure steady white.

DANCING TO THE TIDE OF TIMES

Under the sea they sway,
the long sea grasses—

back and forth they swing
to the count
of countless tides.

I drift on the sea's skin
a momentary nobody
above the stalks'
eternal pendulation.

FULL MOON,

be a discus tonight.
Arms held high,
I'll clasp your light,
spin, hurl,
and make heaven ignite.

WINDS

Music

Aeolus strikes his chimes,
a lone spar sways
on metronome tides
marking the beat
of siren lullabies.

Dancing

The moonlight cuts
a swath of sea
and shines on ripples—
spellbound Bacchae,
their flickering torches,
their wine-dark ecstasy.

Writing

A hollow hush—
blank page after a breeze—
wayward words gather
to take wing at next gust.

Running

Mocking breaths ruffle
the dusky robe of Autumn,
fleeting feet stir
leaves on the path.

Swimming

My cresting head
broaches the sea's skin—
a flash of vision
and the rush of inspiration.

DIVINATION

On this sacred night
I, the dervish of discus,
spin in the dark,

a dancing vortex,
and launch each disc
at the final strophe.

I hurl votive gyres,
sacrifice to the stars,
earth-ripped geomancy—
clairvoyance of scars.

FIRE

Burnt offerings are still found
from Philip the Second's pyre—
animal bones, corners of cloth,
pottery shards, fruit parts
transformed by smoke and fire
to journey with the King:
all things necessary
for delight in Hades,
blessed by flame.

At the fireplace,
a farmer's hand explodes
after too much wine
and a bad idea:
salamander skin sloughs
off thick dripping digits,
serum blisters burst
and weep for a hand
sent oversoon to greet
the Macedonian king.

TRIPOD

Golden-wheeled tripods
forged on Vulcan's anvil
whirl about Olympus
to serve immortal guests.
At Bronze Age Pylos,
found clay tablets
account in Linear B
for every tripod
in Nestor's palace fort.
Tripods were for victory
at music and sport
and for a priestess
poised to see the future.

Half a mile above the sea
there's smoke rising from the chimney
of an ancestral village home
where my cousin cooks
on an iron tripod.
For three hundred years
the house has stood
high on this rock,
stone locked to stone,
walls without mortar
holding back rain and wind.
My grandfather was born here
and his grandfather before him.
Each epoch's midwife
ushers in a life
kept warm by the fire
where boiling incantations
rise from a pot
placed on a tripod.

NOSTOS

Above the sea clouds, the plane climbs,
cuts through mist and wind
to where the sun shines
on cloud city rising
from the shores of cloud lake.

There's a weasel
shaping into a humpback
that spouts in the harbor,
distant domed cathedrals
flanked by castle towers,
and, far off, fog-bricked walls
keep giant Michelin men at bay.

By midday, sea and sky
meld into a common hue—
horizon absorbed
in a seamless tableau—

out the airplane's oval window
ragged clouds in the foreground
crisscross the chimeric view,
suddenly there's my island
levitating, in sumptuous blue.

FROM AN AIRPLANE

A black winter sea
rolling like film stock,
reel, shutter, reel.
I project a night scene
on the dark screen below.

We're approaching from the lee;
waves without crests,
only the onyx oscillations
of swells streaked by spindrift strands.

I pan across this mystic scene—
my own *auteur*, disembodied,
oblivious to the jolting plane
and the pilot saying,
"We'll take another pass
at the landing strip."

Now black sea-screen
looms even closer,
wings see-saw
in gale-force winds:
landing gear is down,
and sweaty palms
grip shaky armrests.

A Jesuit scholar wrote:
"movies are for the masses
what theology is
for the elite."

The plane's wheels
touch the tarmac,
its wings now even,
a cross of salvation
for sinner or elect.
I mumble a prayer of thanks
as runway markers roll past
like credits at the end
of the final reel.

II.
TIME WITHOUT END

AIGALEO METRO STATION

Riding the Athens underground
whose tracks run alongside
the ancient road that starts
at the Keramikos Gate
and leads to the site
of the Eleusinian mysteries,
a young woman gets off the train
and tapping her white cane
from the platform to the escalator,
steps on a moving metal tread
rising to the chill
of a winter afternoon
and the strip of Sacred Way
unearthed before her.
She cannot see its curbs,
its dirt and stone roadbed
and inlaid wheel ruts
from countless carts and chariots,
now covered by a Plexiglas canopy,
or partake in the unknown rites
of the cult's secret creed—
descent, search, ascent:
this blind Kore
rising from the underworld.

AT THE ALTAR OF THE TWELVE GODS
Athens Agora, Northwest Perimeter

It's hidden amongst the acanthus fronds,
flowering oleander, wild olive,
plane and pine trees—plant life so thick
there's always shade, when the sun is high,
and a darker dusk, like now,
when guards blow their whistles
at closing time.

Concealed in this verdure— all that remains
of the Altar of the Twelve Gods,
the starting point from which
all ancient roads were measured—
is the southwest corner,
bordered by a cement and stone wall,
beyond which the greater part of the shrine
lies buried beneath the tracks
of the Athens-Piraeus electric railway.

Eleos, the goddess of pity,
was also worshipped here,
a place of asylum for renegades,
including me, trying now to steal
a few extra minutes
to linger at the altar
before the whistle blowers throw me out.

Light raindrops rattle the leaf skins,
a nightingale sings, mourning doves coo,
and nearby church bells toll;
but loudest is the noise
of the public transport train
above the hidden stones

of this ancient hub,
each day bearing
thousands of passengers
over the buried altar
where unknowingly, for a moment,
they become holy, blessed
by the aura of this sacred place.

PALM SUNDAY
Courtyard of the National Archeological Museum

Palm trees line the path
to the sanctum door—
tall burnished trunks,
flowing crested fronds
that bend and scatter
hosannas
as awestruck pilgrims
emerge into light
from this miracle of Athena.

8 P.M. IN THE BRITISH MUSEUM

That heifer lowing at the skies

Night skies shed darkness
through the roof window
into the dim room,
empty but for cream colored blocks
suspended by shadows.

With the procession
of churning hooves,
sandaled believers in restless dress

move in a rectangular reel,
a frieze of floating stone,
nighttime pilgrims that approach their gods
and do not smile.

HADRIAN STREET

It originates in the oldest quarter of Athens
"the ancient city of Theseus,"
and at the imperial arch
erected in his honor
winds into the new "city of Hadrian
and not of Theseus"—
so the architrave inscriptions proclaim.

Today the street is stormed
by a sudden shower.

Once you could dash
to the emperor's library,
his gift to his beloved city,
of hundred-column fame,
and linger as raindrops tumble
from rooftops, balcony floors, awnings,
to join gutter currents,
and scent the summer air.

SERIFOS

Her turn on the tooth,
one Graiai whistles
a wind song that whips
empty tables, folded chairs
in the frozen square facing
King Polydectes' palace,
now Serifos' town hall.

Down the stone steps
before its portals
a beer can bounces—
and the footsteps
of invisible Perseus:
a severed head
strapped to his back.

FORT LARISSA AT ARGOS

Battlements like birds' nests
gathered piece by piece
from the temple stones of Greece.
Stolen, carved and joined:
centuries of sacrilege, mortar and blood
a thousand feet above Argos Bay,
where dolphins ferry souls
of Argive, Roman, Frank, Venetian, Turk.

DRAKANON, IKARIA

Flying east toward Ionia
the plane lunges in wind gusts
like Phaeton, astray,
lashing his chargers.
It dips and sways
with equine exuberance,
banks suddenly starboard,
where at Ikaria's tip,
on the high ground,
limestone blocks form a round tower
that glistens at first light.
It's Drakanon's shining keep,
a rising colossus like the thigh of Zeus
that gave birth to Bacchus.
Theocritus concurs—
Dionysus was born here,
and at the cape's shore
frothy sweat from Helian horses
crests on the surf.

MYSTRAS

A few miles west of the Spartan plain,
built on a high cliff, a Byzantine city
reaches to the sky—
almond shaped Mystras
also called Little Constantinople.
Here beside its ravaged walls
one draws in air
that Helen once breathed,
a drug evoking
time without end.
And below—what the town scholar
Plethon must have seen
while writing of immortal souls
joined to human bodies,
as he looked down
on the valley of Eurotas
and the path that Paris took
with his prize, headlong to the sea.

THE ANTIKYTHERA SHIPWRECK

They thought he was crazy,
that first diver
looking for a sponge,
as he broke to the surface
and told of a bronze arm
stuck in the seabed.

It was Bion's arm.
Later they found his feet,
corrugated cloak,
left hand and head—
painted eye whites' stare,
long beard, tangled hair.

Bion of the Scythian tribe.
Bion of the diatribe.
Bion a sage of Greece.
A sculptor's masterpiece!
Just south of the Peloponnese
Bion's parts rest in peace.

POSEIDON'S REVENGE

Nameless bronze people,
their bodies cast
from an ancient world,
survived the sea intact:
the shadow boxer
practicing his punches
with fists wrapped
in himantes straps,
an ephebe posed
in a dance position
his torso striking
a sensuous sigma,
an athlete standing tall
holding a scythe-shaped
strigilis to scrape the mix
of grit, olive oil and sweat
off the muscles he trained.
For two thousand years
the sea was kind
to these forgotten figurines,
bronze, barely a foot tall
and buried in the sand
near the Antikythera island seabed.

But the life-size heroes
of Troy carved in marble
and en route to be grouped
in an Italian's villa grotto
reveal a divine vengeance.
Poseidon, nemesis to great Odysseus,
spilled his sea bile
on the Ithacan's stone skin.
The hero's face is pockmarked,

his body, tunic and peaked cap
pitted by the stone-eating
creatures of the sea—
the god's retribution
to the man who blinded
his son Polyphemus.
So too the fate of Achilles,
whose drowned likeness
was found next to the wily Nobody.
We know it's Thetis' son
from what remains
of his long unruly hair,
the banner insignia
that frames a brine-blistered face,
girding a nape
scarred by barnacle acne.
His desecration of Hector's corpse,
one of the world's great war crimes,
was so grievous that the gods
intervened and decreed
a miraculous *beau mort*
for the slain Trojan,
while his slayer's image
was left to lie prone in the seabed
to be eaten by sea worms.

THE PRINCE OF ASINE

Along the coast of Argos bay
it was caught by westerlies
and sank at Point Iria
on its way to trade
at Tiryns, Argos and Asine,
its cargo of pottery
spread for centuries on the seabed,
now on display
in the Spetses island museum.

The ship came from Cyprus
at the time of the Trojan War,
and was wrecked a few miles west
of Asine, a city Homer mentions
once and only once in the Iliad.
Here three thousand years later
Crown Prince Gustav
joined a team of excavators
that hauled thirty tons
of pot shards to Sweden;
and twenty years later
a Greek prince of poetry,
George Seferis, came to look
for the lost King of Asine—
lost among the pot shards,
lost among the site's Cyclopean walls,
lost amidst the myriad names
and places listed in the Iliad;
and found only κενο:
emptiness, desolation, a void.

JUNCTION
Domokos rail yard near Volos

A train stop at this rail yard,
the last stop on flat land,
where electricity ends,
and an old line locomotive waits
to pull the wagons over Othrys mountain.
The diesel engine slides along a strip of track,
past decaying boxcars, an ancient water tower,
piled rusty rails, and warped pylons.
Its buffers tap those
of the lead coach it will convey,
and after a brakeman checks the coupling,
it starts to climb the mountain.

Out the window to the right
are the stones of Othrys' ridge,
on the left, the Plain of Thessaly—
a quilt of green and brown,
fertile and fallow farmland;
then in and out of tunnels,
through pine forests
and past a wartime pillbox.

This is the battleground
of the ten-year titanomachy,
where the sons of Uranus
fought the gods of Olympus
and where Germans crossed
on mountain trails,
to invade and devour
the ancient land.
But like Kronos, who swallowed
a rock instead of his child

and was pelted with boulders
from hundred-handed giants,
they ended with nothing but stones.

MIST CLOUD

A fierce Northern blow
like an inverse Sisyphus
pushed a cloud of mist
slowly down the South slope
of Mount Atheras,
rolling to low ground,
a ghost avalanche;
the cotton lava
bore down on me
then stopped,
and, through a rent
in the thick curtain,
suddenly I could see
clear winter sky,
and the first star.

SPARTO

It flowers bright yellow
along the hillsides
each island Spring.
Nubs of gold cap
tall thin shafts;
Homer's *sparto*,
called Spanish Broom in English.
When the shrub's in bloom,
gilding rock ridges
with sunshine hues,
picture a field of daffodils
tilted on its side,
and a long line of poets
rejoicing since ancient times.

III.
TWICE TOLD

WEREWOLVES OF ARCADIA

Pastoral Arcadia, a place
of idyllic landscapes,
blithe shepherds and maidens,
but not always so....

Before the Flood
the Arcady of poets
was home to werewolves
born even before the moon.

Foremost of these was King Lycaon,
changed into a wolf-man
after he sacrificed a child
at the altar of Zeus

then feasted upon it at table,
a sacrilege that so enraged the god
that he purged the earth
with a great flood

which only Deucalion (son of Prometheus),
his wife Pyrra, and Arcus, eponym
for the fabled realm, survived
to toss the stones that restored our race.

When the water receded,
the land became werewolf free,
transformed and sublime....
Yet Poussin's painting comes to mind:

a bucolic rustic scene,
handsome shepherds posed
before a grave's *memento mori*—
"I too am here, even in Arcadia."

APOLLO RETURNS FROM THE HEBRIDES

On a steep path
from Temple Tholos
to the gym colonnade
mists writhe down
from Mount Parnassos
to curtain the distant shrine.

At this spring moment,
when Apollo returns to Delphi,
two gods meet.

Reason embraces passionate Dionysus,
the Winter guardian, lord
of dreams and drunken fevers…

When the rains stop,
a breath, wildflower sweet,
lifts the fog
before Apollo's temple
unveiling the pilgrim queue
waiting for Pythia to sing.

THE EPIPHANY
Iliad books 3 and 22

No web of peace,
Helen weaves on purple cloth
the bloody sequel
to her rape from home.

At the loom she works,
the linen report
of brave lives lost—

her glory, her renown.

Iris, winged herald obscure,
whispers a message
only souls can hear.

The Queen of Sparta
quits her purple art
and veiled in white
follows Iris to grieve
at the ramparts—

her shame, her sorrow.

Andromache weaves
flower hems to purple cloth.
Struck by sudden dread,
she drops her shuttle,
dashes to the walls
and sees her sister's work—

widows, orphans, slaves.

PENELOPE'S CRAFT

Crossing the warp waves,
plying between frame shores,
the weft its wake,
her shuttle weaves
a winding sheet
that sleight hands
dissolve at night.

And when surly guests
plunder her craft,
the loom beam,
on destiny's tide
bends to a hand bow.

THE SHADOW IN THE CAVE

Odysseus, a captive, watches
as sunset halos the space
between cavern lips
and Cyclops' stone door.

Deep in the earth's belly
Nobody's cannibal host
makes a fire that casts
shadows on the wall.

In these darting shadows
Nobody discerns the form
of a fire-spear for blinding
the single eye of savagery.

So Nobody, cued by a shadow,
slips from the cave
strapped to a sheep's belly,
rises into daylight
and stands, Somebody bold,
crowing his *kleos* to taunt
his captor's father, Poseidon.

SPINNING AND WEAVING

Plasma flax dressed
on a high distaff
drawn and twisted
into a double helix;
this yarn of life
is fixed as warp
to cosmic looms,
each hanging braid
a puppet string
that the shuttle laces
with wefts of fate
that stir the strands
of molecule bases.

DANTE AT THE DRIVE-IN
Purgatorio, Canto X

The wandering rocks
weave like waves
on the pilgrim's
moonlit path.
Narrow to navigate
this perilous pass,
he twists
his solid shape
through a scar
in the stone face.

Before him, day lit,
a desolate ledge
facing the white wall
of visible speech.
Shining sculpted
angels, kings, horsemen
sing, dance, talk
to eyes incredulous
to ears ecstatic
that say yes and no!

The pilgrim stands awestruck
as next a parade
of condemned souls passes;
hunched and reeling
hauling stones
strapped to their backs.
His kind heart is saddened
seeing these spirits,
bent by their burden of sin
and forbidden to see.

DANTE AT THE DINER

In the dark forest of towers
the wandering pilgrim is lost.
Pelted by rain and sleet,
he enters the diner
(a dripping comedic diviner)
feeling vague unease;
when he looks about
this is what he sees...

First a solitary woman
skirted in a spotted hide
smiles with bold abandon
shameless, beckoning eyed.

Next a man, his skin
suggesting the lion's land
tells tales no one
can understand.

A third he spies
howling at a mirror's peek
of a lupus rash
erupting on her cheek.

The pilgrim turns
and bolts for the door.
Swiftly runs into the night,
for he had visited Hell before.

A TRUE SEA YARN

A captain died one wintry night
on shipboard, with a cargo
of tar and lumber, heading north
from Trinidad and Tobago.

His crew refused to tarp him
and toss him to the tide,
instead they welded oil drums
then set the bier topside.

The ship steamed on through snow and sleet
day after wintry day;
the cold that drove the crew below
kept the captain from decay.

Until one night in St. John's port
amidst a snowy squall
floodlights shone on the jib boom line
lowering the metal pall,

as stevedores along the dock
welcomed the honored dead
and, standing at attention, raised
the helmets from their heads.

Now the captain and this modest yarn
are at their final rest.
Reader, are you sadder and wiser—
like a certain Wedding-Guest?

IV.
STONE SONG

TWO SIREN STATUES

flank the grave stele.
Sorrow-sculpted faces,
wings Medusa-struck.

They sing a stone song.
Notes like pebble tears
fall on the dead man's ears.

HERO'S BURIAL

A.J.T., who hid a Jewish friend from the Nazis.
Honored by Yad Vashem

Summoned to an empty church,
I saw you dead.
Kissed your cold bald head
scented with iodine wash.
This holy place was fitting—
beneath the icon eyes,
the utter solitude—
for one who sheltered
innocent blood
from certain death,
setting forth
to the dark gate alone,
a hoplite of life.

BIKES

My father loved to bring bikes
home to his kids on their birthdays:
scent of new rubber tires—
faint, acrid, fragrant;
fresh paint on frames and fenders—
royal blue, olive green, old gold, cardinal red.

Sometimes he'd take a ride
on the big red-framed bike
and my brothers and I
would follow behind
on the blue, green and gold ones;
up and down the long block,
summer evenings as the sun went down.

It was a long ride for my father
to reach this quiet street
in a quiet Ohio town
coming from wartime Greece
where the basement of his father's house
was the town bomb shelter.

He didn't ride like other Ohio dads;
he pedalled in dress oxfords without socks,
solemn, bald headed—
we were happy riding with him
but kept a reverent distance and kept quiet too.

Once after a ride
he told us half in Greek
half in English, how his mentor,
President Eisenhower's heart doctor,
Professor Paul Dudley White
would ride his bike each day
to the Harvard hospital.

And sometimes, after biking,
we'd drive to the store
for a half-gallon of ice cream.
It was dark outside
by the time we sat at table
to scoop out the treat.

But he never spoke to us
(I overheard it)
about the children of Athens
he saw dead on the street
their bellies bloated from starvation,
mornings when he went to work
that first frigid winter of occupation.

My father died of Alzheimer's disease.
In his last days
he smiled the child's smile
that we would smile
when we followed him
on our bikes.

During a lucid moment,
just before the end,
he told me of the time
during the war
when Germans came to his house
and stole his bike.

"It was a French racing cycle,
its frame and fenders were painted white."

SAILING TO ALZHEIMER'S

I close the barred door
turning the lock
that keeps the old man
from wandering to the rocks.

Father, who reached out
his hand to me
through the grate
like a home-bound shipmate
slipping down Scylla's maw.

DREAMING OF THE DEAD

Mindful of his madness
I kept a close watch
and locked the gate.

Yet I saw him far away—
short portly bald man
walking in a mist…

Darkness, then closer vision's view—
the short portly bald man
face down in a ditch…

Do the dead die twice
before harboring at first light?

THE IMPATIENT

"It's time for me,
my friends spellbound
in this room without a sound.
How they weep and smile at once—
a gesture of hope.
And as I grasp for breath
I do my very best
to rise and live
for those at my bedside.
I need my life tonight
to be gracious to my guests
but it waits at the open window
impatient to greet
the stars and moon."

TONIGHT THE MOON LOOKS LIKE
AGAMEMNON'S DEATH MASK

Alive now,
peeking through the eye slits
he looks down
at the ferry steaming
across Homer's Aegean,
where on deck, Helen from Ohio
sits huddled in a sleeping bag
staring in wonder at the face
of the wide-ruling king.
No war prize
or fabled bride of spears,
but beautiful in the moonbeams
she captures men's eyes
as Paris from Patras
and Achilles from Argos
admire her from afar
and long to coax her
from Atreides' entrancing light.

SHE STOPPED AT THE MOON

on her way to heaven.
And I kept a vigil,
at grief's cloister, by the sea,

until compassionate skies
revealed the lid of her eye
broaching the horizon.
Swimming, I followed her gleam
until I could go no more.

Then prostrate on the shore,
I saw the vision of her smile,
heard her song, a heartbeat deathless
until the last tides whisper,
"it's ok, it's ok, it's ok."

STONY BEACH

A soul inside each stone
tossed by the sea.
Only the divine waves
that wash and sanctify
can shake these votaries
of the lithosphere
crawling toward a bethel.

V.

THE DISQUIETING
MUSE

SPARAGMOS

Chet Baker is running down Bridgewater Street.
He just got paid
after a gig at the Trident Restaurant
where there's a beautiful view
of San Francisco Bay and Angel Island.

But he's not enjoying the view,
he's trying to escape
from a gang of thugs:
minions of a Dionysian drug lord
to whom he owes money.

Crazed like Maenads,
they take his pay,
smash his face,
ruin his embouchure
so badly he can't play
for three years.

Instead he visits the underworld,
geezing each day on smack,
painting houses, pumping gas,
pawning his horn for dope money.
It floats down a river
along with his ripped, severed head.

Chet tells how two black guys
saved him: chased off the punks,
then took him to a hospital.
They must have been at the gig
and heard how he could play—

how, as he tapped the piston keys
and sang in his soft tenor
he could move rocks and trees,
tame wild beasts,
make fish jump from the sea.

MOSQUITO

On Greek funerary vases
the dead man's soul
is often portrayed
as a small, flitting, winged figure
rising from his mouth and hovering
over his likeness, like a mosquito—

like the mosquito that bit
Rupert Brooke on the lip
as he read to friends his sonnets
that revel in the coming
of a war whose trench fighting
he would never live to see—

a tiny flying bane,
perhaps from the underworld,
that jabbed poison to his lip
and cut short the voice
of those gallant war poems,
or any chance to amend them
into songs of sorrow.

THE POET

On most days he was late
to his work at the ministry,
once crisply scolded:
"Mr. Cavafy, you are
not giving satisfaction."

And a curious assistant
peeking through the keyhole,
spied him, seated at his desk
talking to himself as
his hands sawed the air.

Ah, but if he liked you,
invited you to his home
above the brothel
("One must pity the girls
but they receive some angels")

he would sit in the shadows
next to the candles burning low
speaking unkindly of his rival:
"No, no that's Palamas whiskey,
for you I have something better."

ANGELO BARDI

In the Bardi chapel
of Santa Croce Basilica
Giotto painted an angel
imprinting the stigmata
on St. Francis.

In the piazza
before the church
a young artist paces alone
having lost all hope
for a "disquieting muse."

When the angel
flies from the chapel
and scuds about the square
the artist sees, for the first time,
how his picture should look.

The young painter, Giorgio de Chirico,
called himself "Angelo Bardi"
when he told how
he painted an enigma
on an autumn afternoon.

TWO BOATS

A painting by his friend
shows Monet at work
on his floating atelier.
Before an easel
balanced on the gunwale
and wearing a straw hat,
"the Raphael of water"
thoughtfully daubs
to capture the light
of a glimmering Seine.
Unlike the fishing cruiser
of the burly author
who wrote powerhouse prose,
this studio boat
saw no moments of drama—
no shooting at sharks
with a tommy gun,
no hunting for subs
in Cuban coves,
no blood on the bridge
from gashed heads and thighs—
although once, in anger,
the artist threw his paints
and brushes overboard.

RESURRECTION

The mosaics of Agia Sophia in Constantinople were plastered over by the Ottoman Turks in 1453, and were restored by a team led by Thomas Whittemore between 1931 and 1938. Yeats's "Sailing to Byzantium" was published in 1926.

Entombed in the mezzanine
under a starlit dome,
the Deesis of Agia Sophia,
a gold mosaic icon, lay
five centuries swathed in gypsum,
its solemn holy faces
by the world unseen.

The gray-haired poet-sage
who wished to come
and kneel before these tessellations
in his tattered mortal dress
would have seen only their desecration
as he prayed from far away
to belong to a bygone age.

And through the augury
of a heart consumed
he saw the gold,
the glistening pieces juxtaposed,
craftsmen on scaffolds,
hammers cracking plaster
resurrecting an artifice of eternity.

THE SUN SETS ON CINEMA HISTORY

The actors would come
in taxis each morning
to this then desolate beach
facing Mount Vardia,
use the cement floor
of the one café there
as rehearsal space,
dance studio and commissary.

Fifty years ago
with the cameras rolling
and Zorba and Basil
dancing arm in arm
before the sea,
no one expected a Greek film
about a peasant and a scholar
to become cinema history.

The café is there still;
on one wall hang stills
from the movie set,
and Vardia looms still
and calico when the sun is high—
then burnished red then grey
that, as night comes on,
fades to black.

THE LAST OF BYRON

His Blood

Three times
he refused to be bled
but "the damn set of butchers"
prevailed and shed
with leech and lancet
the soldier poet's
tithe to liberty.

His Spirit

He screamed "A Christi"
and clenched his fists—
ichor flows on Easter day.
Waiting outside, a tempest:
Zeus thundering at the door
claims his passion, his spirit
rising in the downpour.

His Body

All eyes upon him,
his sacrifice a promise,
torsoed and featured
like fallen Adonis
with cloven feet
that traveled ancient lands
melding Apollo with Satyros Pan.

THE POET IS ROUSED FROM A DREAM

by a thunderstorm.
His house is his head.
Lightning flashes the windows.
Words rattle the panes.
He gets from his bed
padding softly downstairs
in pajamas, on bare feet,
sits at a table and writes
words the storm whispers—
the poem of his house.

HIPPOCAMPUS
(locus of creativity in the human brain)

The mother of muses
brings her tykes
to magic Mount Helicon
so they can play
with a flying horse.

As the children romp,
Mnemosyne strolls off,
thoughtful and serene,
down a path that leads
to river Hippocrene.

Suddenly darting her godhand
in quicksilver currents,
she captures a white seahorse
and carries away the memento
to give to those flighty girls.

THE LINES

On rail tracks with no beginning and no end
a serpent engine clears the bend.
With cars in tow, each rattle and rasp
proclaims the lines the train wheels grasp.
It writes them too with shaky scrawl
and punctuates with whistle call.
What's to be penned in snake train hand?
Eternity lies ahead, behind lies empty land.

THE SORROW OF HERAKLES

Toward the end,
sculptors made him weary,
his stone face pensive.
Herakles' image, like his labors,
reveals the soul of Greece,
from Archaic zeal
to classical severity.
Yet the epitrapezios bronze
that his descendant Alexander
carried on campaign
has a look of sorrow.
The world was not enough.

Herakles' last Greek likeness,
the Farnese, carved by Lysippos,
shows him with bowed head
renouncing his massive brawn,
his mighty club.

NOTES

VIEW FROM THE EMERGENCY ROOM

P. 4 "Incident on Greek Independence Day." Greek Independence Day is celebrated on March 25th of each year. The foustanella is pleated skirt garb worn by Greek men in the 17th and 18th century.

P. 8 "Falcons at Sunset." Eleonora of Arborea (1347-1404), Sardinia's most renowned heroine.

P. 11 "Dolphin." When Dionysus set sail for Naxos, some say from Ikaria island, the ship's crew had mischief in store.

P. 14 "Late Laps on the Island." "There was a strange call from the dark trees to the east of the house....It was very high pitched, repeated at regular intervals: Kew, Kew, Kew....' 'What is it?' 'The Scops owl.'" John Fowles, *The Magus*, revised edition (Little, Brown, 1977), Chapter 17.

P. 15 "When Water Turns to Wine." Dionysus, conceived in his mother's womb and incubated in Zeus' thigh, is known as the "twice born god." Dio-nysus means Zeus-thigh in Greek. According to Robert Graves, Dionysus' mother Semele is usually explained as a form of Selene (moon).

P. 16 "Octopus." According to the *Penguin Dictionary of Symbols*, the square "is the symbol of the created universe" (p. 912); and "The most usual wheel has always been eight-spoked...and eight spokes symbolize regeneration and renewal" (p. 1100). Of course the sideways figure eight is the mathematical symbol for infinity.

P. 22 "Divination." Geomancy is divination by means of fissures or holes in the earth or geographic features.

P. 23 "Fire." Philip II's tomb was discovered on November 8, 1977 at Vergina, Greek Macedonia. Artifacts preserved and recovered from his funeral pyre are on display at the site's museum.

P. 24 "Tripod." According to Homer, *Iliad* 18, 434-440 (Fagles translation), Hephaestus built 20 golden wheeled robotic tripods that whisked about the halls of Mt. Olympus to serve the gods. The Linear B script was used by the Mycenaean Greeks between 1450-1200 B.C. It was deciphered in the 1950's A.D.

P. 25 "Nostos." The ancient Greek concept of homecoming.

P. 26 "From an Airplane." Neil P. Hurley SJ, author of *Theology Through Film* (Harper and Row 1970).

TIME WITHOUT END

P. 31 "Aigaleo Metro Station." The Eleusinian Mysteries celebrated Persephone's annual emergence from the underworld. Kore is an epithet for Persephone.

P. 34 "Palm Sunday." "Certain museums are so essential, with collections so central to the heritage of the entire human race, they seem to belong to the whole world. The Athens Archeological Museum is just such a place." *USA Today*, Oct. 22, 1992.

P. 37 "Serifos." The Graiai were two (some say three) crone divinities who shared a single eye and a single tooth between them. Medusa was the only mortal Gorgon. After Perseus decapitated her, he carried her head to display and thus petrify his enemies. Also, when Medusa was beheaded Pegasus (symbol of poetry) and the giant Khrysaor sprang from the neck wound.

P. 38 "Fort Larissa at Argos." Greek temples were often demolished during the Middle Ages so that their stones could be recycled for use in building forts and churches.

P. 39 "Drakanon, Ikaria." Theocritus writing in the 3rd century B.C. is best known as the creator of pastoral poetry. The circular tower on the Eastern promontory of Ikaria is thought to date from Hellenistic times.

P. 40 "Mystras." Neoplatonist philosopher George Gemiston Plethon lived in Mystras until his death in 1452. Plethon helped shape the course of the Italian Renaissance when he visited Florence in 1439. Cosimo d'Medici attended his lectures. Other Byzantine "émigré" scholars who influenced Renaissance thought were: John Argyropoulos (Da Vinci attended his lectures), Janus Lascaris, Theodore Gaza and Demetrios Chalkokondyles.

P. 41 "The Antikythera Shipwreck." Sunken artifacts from the 1st century B.C. were discovered off the coast of Antikythera island in October 1900 in the way described. Bion of Borysthenes c.325-350 B.C. was a cynic philosopher and author of "The Diatribes."

P. 42 "Poseidon's Revenge." Among the sunken artifacts found at the site of the Antikythera wreck (see note above) are a group of bronze figurine depictions of everyday citizens of antiquity and also a marble statue group of Trojan War heroes similar in many ways to the statuary that decorated the grotto of Emperor Tiberius' villa at Sperlonga. Jacques Cousteau and his team aboard the oceanographic vessel Calypso assisted in the salvage of these treasures. Cousteau's exploration of the wreck is filmed in the 1978 documentary "Diving for Roman Plunder."

P. 44 "The Prince of Asine." From 1920-1924 Crown Prince Gustav of Sweden participated in the archaeological excavation of the Mycenaean city of Asine located on the coast of the Argolid, a short distance from the Point Iria wreck. Most of the thirty tons of excavated pot shards are now kept in the Asine Collection at the University of Uppsala. In 1940, poet George Seferis memorialized his visit to the site in his poem "The King of Asine."

P. 45 "Junction." The Titanomachy between the male Titans and the Olympian gods lasted for 10 years. Zeus freed the 100-handed giants from Tartarus and recruited them to fight against the Titans.

TWICE TOLD

P. 52 "Apollo Returns From the Hebrides." Apollo allowed his younger brother Dionysus to stay at Delphi for the three winter months while he vacationed in the land of the Hyperboreans. There's a vase painting dated about 400 B.C. that shows Apollo and Dionysus in Delphi holding out their hands to one another.

P. 55 "The Shadow in the Cave." I've always wondered if Plato conceived his theory of forms after reading Book IX of *The Odyssey*. *Kleos* is the ancient Greek concept of fame, glory and renown.

P. 59 "A True Sea Yarn." This tale was told to me by one of the old salts who drink and play cards at Ikaria's cafés overlooking the sea.

STONE SONG

P. 64 "Hero's Burial." AJT is my father. Yad Vashem, established in 1953, is Israel's official memorial to the Jewish victims of the holocaust. "On July 27th 1988, Yad Vashem recognized Alexandros Tripoulas as Righteous Among the Nations."

P. 67 "Sailing to Alzheimer's." *The Odyssey* Book 12 lines 275-282.

P. 72 "Stony Beach." The Penguin *Dictionary of Symbols* defines bethel: "sacred stones venerated…as manifestations of the divine presence" and gives as examples Jacob's pillow and the omphalos at Delphi. Elsewhere it states that: "stones were not lifeless masses, living stones fell from heaven and they remain alive after their fall."

THE DISQUIETING MUSE

P. 79 "Angelo Bardi." The angel of the Bardi chapel, Santa Croce Basilica, Florence. Di Chirico used the pen name "Angelo Bardi" in an article describing his "revelation" in the Piazza Santa Croce that inspired his first metaphysical painting, *The Enigma of an Autumn Afternoon*.

P. 83 "The Last of Byron." Byron died at Messolongi at quarter past six in the evening on April 19, 1824, Easter Day. According to William Parry, "The pestilent sirocco was blowing a hurricane, and the rain was falling with almost tropical violence."

P. 85 "Hippocampus." The hippocampus is a seahorse-shaped white-matter component of the human brain. It plays an important role in the formation of episodic memory and emotional responses. The Hippocrene spring, considered the source of poetic inspiration, is located on Mt. Helicon and sprang forth when Pegasus kicked at a rock in the mountainside. Mnemosyne, the Titan goddess of memory, gave birth to the nine muses. Mt. Helicon is sacred to the muses.

P. 86 "The Lines." I lived on a circus train for a year.

ABOUT THE AUTHOR

Since 2009 JOHN TRIPOULAS has served as the general sur-geon on the Greek island of Ikaria, where his father and paternal grandparents were born. John was born and grew up in Cleve-land, Ohio, but as a teenager attended high school in Athens, Greece. He was graduated from Oberlin College with a BA in English literature and subsequently received an MD from Ath-ens University Medical School. His maternal grandfather was the Greek poet and Olympic athlete Demetrios Golemis, whose poems John has translated into English in a volume titled *De-molished Souls* (Cosmos Press, 2011).

Author Photo by Iannis Falkonis

R. Nemo Hill - *When Men Bow Down* (2012)

W. Nick Hill - *And We'd Understand Crows Laughing* (2012),
    Blue Nocturne (2016)

Eric Hoffman - *Life At Braintree* (2008), *The American Eye* (2011),
    By the Hours (2013), *Forms of Life* (2015)

Roald Hoffmann - *Something That Belongs To You* (2015)

James Hogan - *Rue St. Jacques* (2005)

Keith Holyoak - *My Minotaur* (2010), *Foreigner* (2012),
    The Gospel According to Judas (2015)

Nancy Kassell - *Text(isles)* (2013)

David M. Katz - *Claims of Home* (2011), *Stanzas on Oz* (2015)

Sherry Kearns - *Deep Kiss* (2013), *The Magnificence of Ruin* (2015)

Marjorie Deiter Keyishian - *Ashes and All* (2015)

Burt Kimmelman - *There Are Words* (2007), *The Way We Live* (2011)

Jill Kelly Koren - *The Work of the Body* (2015)

Ralph La Charity - *Farewellia a la Aralee* (2014)

Pamela L. Laskin - *Plagiarist* (2012)

Owen Lewis - *Sometimes Full of Daylight* (2013), *Best Man* (2015)

Richard Luftig - *Off The Map* (2006)

Austin MacRae - *The Organ Builder* (2012)

Mario Markus - *Chemical Poems-One For Each Element* (2013)

J. Morris - *The Musician, Approaching Sleep* (2006)

Patricia Monaghan - *Mary-A Life in Verse* (2014)

Rick Mullin - *Soutine* (2012), *Coelacanth* (2013),
    Sonnets on the Voyage of the Beagle (2014), *Stignatz* (2015)

Fred Muratori - *A Civilization* (2014)

Robert Murphy - *Not For You Alone* (2004), *Life in the Ordovician*
(2007),
    From Behind The Blind (2013)

Pam O'Brien - *The Answer To Each Is The Same* (2012)

Peter O'Leary - *A Mystical Theology of the Limbic Fissure* (2005)

Sharon Olinka - *Old Ballerina Club* (2016)

Bea Opengart - *In The Land* (2011)

David A. Petreman - *Candlelight in Quintero-bilingual ed.* (2011)

Paul Pines - *Reflections in a Smoking Mirror* (2011),
  New Orleans Variations & Paris Ouroboros (2013),
  Fishing on the Pole Star (2014)
  Message from the Memoirist (2015)

Quanita Roberson - *Soul Growing-Wisdom for thirteen year old boys
  from men around the world* (2015)

William Schickel - *What A Woman* (2007)

Don Schofield - *In Lands Imagination Favors* (2014)

David Schloss - *Behind the Eyes* (2005),
  Reports from Babylon and Beyond (2015)

Daniel Shapiro - *The Red Handkerchief and other poems* (2014)

Murray Shugars - *Songs My Mother Never Taught Me* (2011),
  Snakebit Kudzu (2013)

Jason Shulman - *What does reward bring you but to bind you to
  Heaven like a slave? (2013)*

Maxine Silverman - *Palimpsest (2014)*

Lianne Spidel & Anne Loveland - *Pairings* (2012),
  A Bird in the Hand (2014)

Olivia Stiffler - *Otherwise, we are safe* (2013)

Carole Stone - *Hurt, the Shadow-the Josephine Hopper poems* (2013)

Nathan Swartzendruber - *Opaque Projectionist* (2009)

Jean Syed - *Sonnets* (2009)

Eileen R. Tabios - *INVENT[ST]ORY Selected Catalog Poems and New
  1996-2015* (2015)

Madeline Tiger - *The Atheist's Prayer* (2010), *From the Viewing Stand* (2011)

James Tolan - *Red Walls* (2011)

Brian Volck - *Flesh Becomes Word* (2013)

Henry Weinfield - *The Tears of the Muses* (2005),
  Without Mythologies (2008), *A Wandering Aramaean* (2012)

Donald Wellman - *A North Atlantic Wall* (2010),
  The Cranberry Island Series (2012)

Sarah White - *The Unknowing Muse* (2014)

Anne Whitehouse - *The Refrain* (2012)
Martin Willetts Jr. - *Secrets No One Must Talk About* (2011)
Tyrone Williams - *Futures, Elections* (2004), *Adventures of Pi* (2011)
Geoffrey Woolf - *Learn to Love Explosives* (2016)
David Almaleck Wolinsky - *The Crane is Flying - Early Poems* (2016)
Kip Zegers - *The Poet of Schools* (2013), *The Pond in Room 318* (2015)

www.dosmadres.com